CATS
SETS II

Oriental Shorthair Cats

Stuart A. Kallen
ABDO & Daughters

visit us at
www.abdopub.com

Published by Abdo & Daughters, 4940 Viking Drive, Suite 622, Edina, Minnesota 55435.
Copyright © 1998 by Abdo Consulting Group, Inc., Pentagon Tower, P.O. Box 36036,
Minneapolis, Minnesota 55435 USA. International copyrights reserved in all countries.
No part of this book may be reproduced in any form without written permission from the
publisher.

Printed in the United States.

Photo credits: Peter Arnold, Inc., Animals Animals

Edited by Lori Kinstad Pupeza

Library of Congress Cataloging-in-Publication Data

Kallen, Stuart A., 1955-
        Oriental shorthair cats / by Stuart A. Kallen.
        p. cm. -- (Cats. Set II)
        Includes index.
        Summary: Describes the physical characteristics, behavior, and life cycle of
        these smart, graceful cats.
        ISBN 1-56239-582-3
        1. Oriental shorthair cat--Juvenile literature. [1. Oriental shorthair cat. 2. Cats.]
        I. Title. II. Series: Kallen, Stuart A., 1955-   Cats. Set II.
        SF449.073K35 1998
        636.8'25--dc20   95-48188
                                                              CIP
                                                              AC

Contents

Lions, Tigers, and Cats

Few animals are as beautiful and graceful as cats. All types of cats are related. From the wild lions of Africa to common house cats, all belong to the family **Felidae**. Wild cats are found almost everywhere. They include cheetahs, jaguars, lynx, ocelots, and **domestic** cats.

Cats were first domesticated around 5,000 years ago in the Middle East. Although tamed by humans, house cats still think and act like their bigger cousins.

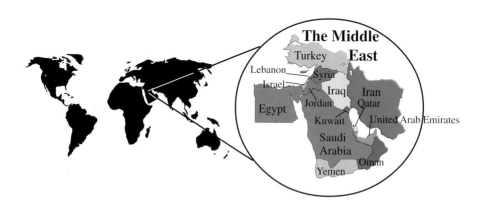

The Middle East

Turkey
Lebanon
Israel
Syria
Iraq
Iran
Qatar
Egypt
Jordan
Kuwait
United Arab Emirates
Saudi Arabia
Oman
Yemen

Coat and Color

Orientals have the short, fine, glossy coats of the Siamese. Their colorings and markings may be as mixed and varied as any **non-pedigree** cat's. There are over 50 colorings and patterns for Oriental shorthair cats.

Orientals may be white, cream, lavender, red, fawn, red and white, cinnamon brown, caramel, blue, or ebony. They may have smoked markings including blue smoke, chestnut smoke, lavender smoke, and others.

They may have tabby markings in all colors with patched, spotted, or ticked tabby patterns. These colors may include red ticked tabby, lavender ticked tabby, chestnut classic tabby, chestnut silver tabby, and others.

Oriental shorthairs may have tortoiseshell—or "tortie"—markings that include silver spotted tortie, cinnamon tortie, and chestnut tortie.

Most Oriental shorthair cats have green, almond-shaped eyes.

White Orientals may have blue eyes. The noses and paw pads usually match the coat color, and range from pink to blue to black.

Oriental shorthairs come in many different colors.

Size

The Oriental shorthair is a medium-sized cat that may weigh between 5 and 10 pounds (2 to 4.5 kg). Their features are exactly the same as Siamese cats. They have long, **lithe**, tubular bodies.

Their legs are long and slender and they have small oval paws. Oriental shorthairs are fine-boned. They have long, tapering, wedge-shaped heads. The ears of the Oriental shorthair cat are large, pointy, and wedge-shaped. They have long whip-like tails.

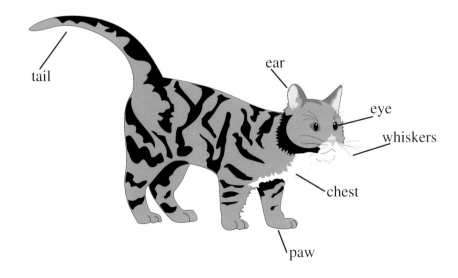

tail

ear

eye

whiskers

chest

paw

Oriental shorthairs have long sleek bodies.

Care

Like any pet, an Oriental shorthair needs a lot of love and attention. They make fine pets. But they still have some of their wild instincts. Cats are natural hunters and do well exploring outdoors.

A **scratching post** where the cat can sharpen its claws saves furniture from damage. A cat buries its waste and should be trained to use a litter box. The box needs to be cleaned every day. Cats lick their coats to stay clean. Oriental shorthair cats are very clean and need little brushing—once a week or less. These cats love to play. A ball, **catnip**, or a loose string will keep a kitten busy for hours.

Cats should be **spayed** or **neutered** unless you are planning to breed them. Females can have dozens of kittens in a year. Males will spray very unpleasant odors indoors and out if not fixed.

Oriental shorthair cats need little brushing.

Feeding

Cats are meat eaters. Hard bones that do not splinter help keep a cat's teeth and mouth clean. Fresh, lean meat is a treat for cats. Water should always be available.

Most cats survive fine on dried cat food. Although they love milk, it might cause cats to become ill. The muscular Oriental shorthair needs a high-protein, well-balanced diet. If it plays outdoors, it might find birds or rodents to eat. Ask a **veterinarian** about the best food for your cat.

Opposite page: Oriental shorthairs need a high-protein diet.

Kittens

A female cat is pregnant for about 65 days. When kittens are born, there may be from two to eight babies. The average Oriental shorthair has five pudgy kittens per litter. Kittens are blind and helpless for the first several weeks. After about three weeks kittens will start crawling and playing.

At this time they may be given cat food. After about a month, kittens will run, wrestle, and play games. A kitten's eye color does not develop until it is six to eight weeks old. If the cat has a **pedigree**, its kittens should be **registered** and given papers at this time. At 10 weeks the kittens are old enough to be sold or given away.

Opposite page: Eye color doesn't develop until the kitten is eight weeks old.

Buying a Kitten

The best place to get an Oriental shorthair cat is from a breeder. Cat shows are also good places to find kittens. Next you must decide if you want a simple pet or a show winner. A basic Oriental can cost $150. Blue-ribbon winners can cost as much as $1,500. When you buy an Oriental shorthair, you should get **pedigree** papers that **register** the animal with the **Cat Fanciers Association**.

When buying a kitten, check it closely for signs of good health. The ears, nose, mouth, and fur should be clean. Its eyes should be bright and clear. The cat should be alert and interested in its surroundings. A healthy kitten will move around with its head held high.

Two Oriental shorthair kittens

Glossary

breed/official breed - a kind of cat, an Oriental shorthair is a breed of cat. An official breed is a breed that is recognized by special cat organizations.

Cat Fanciers Association (CFA) - a group that sets the standards for the breeds of cats.

catnip - the dried leaves and stems of a plant of the mint family, used as a stuffing for cats' toys because cats are stimulated by and drawn to its strong smell.

domestic/domesticated - tamed or adapted to home life.

Felidae - Latin name given to the cat family.

lithe - flexible, bending and moving easily.

neutered - a male cat that is neutered cannot get a female cat pregnant.

non-pedigree - an animal without record of its ancestors.

pedigree - a record of an animal's ancestors.

register - to add a cat to an official record of a breed.

scratching post - a post for a cat to scratch on, which is usually made out of wood or covered with carpet, so the cat can wear down its nails.

spayed - a female cat that is spayed cannot have kittens.

veterinarian - an animal doctor.

Internet Sites

All About Cats
http://w3.one.net/~mich/index.html
See pictures of cats around the net, take a cat quiz to win prizes, and there is even a cat advice column. This is a fun and lively site.

Cat Fanciers Website
http://www.fanciers.com/
Information on breeds, shows, genetics, breed rescue, catteries and other topics. This is a very informative site, including clubs and many links.

Cats Homepage
http://www.cisea.it/pages/gatto/meow.htm
Page for all cat lovers. Cat photo gallery, books and more. This site has music and chat rooms, it's a lot of fun.

Cats Cats Cats
http://www.geocities.com/Heartland/Hills/5157/
This is just a fun site with pictures of cats, links, stories, and other cat stuff.

These sites are subject to change. Go to your favorite search engine and type in CATS for more sites.

PASS IT ON

Tell Others Something Special About Your Pet

To educate readers around the country, pass on interesting tips about animals, maybe a fun story about your animal or pet, and little unknown facts about animals. We want to hear from you!

To get posted on ABDO & Daughters website, E-mail us at "animals@abdopub.com"

Index